Mississippi

Rich Smith

Visit us at
www.abdopublishing.com

Published by ABDO Publishing Company, 8000 West 78th Street, Suite 310, Edina, Minnesota 55439 USA. Copyright ©2010 by Abdo Consulting Group, Inc. International copyrights reserved in all countries. No part of this book may be reproduced in any form without written permission from the publisher. The Checkerboard Library™ is a trademark and logo of ABDO Publishing Company.

Printed in the United States.

Editor: John Hamilton
Graphic Design: Sue Hamilton
Cover Illustration: Neil Klinepier
Cover Photo: iStock Photo
Interior Photo Credits: AirPhoto/Jim Wark, Alabama Department of Archives & History, Alamy, Alexandre de Batz, AP Images, Bill Stark, Coca-Cola Company, Comstock, Corbis, Dr. Jimmy S. Emerson, Getty, Granger Collection, Gunter Küchler, iStock Photo, Library of Congress, Metro-Goldwyn-Mayer, Mile High Maps, Mississippi Braves, Mississippi Rebels, Mississippi RiverKings, Mississippi Sea Wolves, Mountain High Maps, Nathan Culpepper, North Wind Picture Archives, One Mile Up, Paramount Pictures, William Steene.
Statistics: State population statistics taken from 2008 U.S. Census Bureau estimates. City and town population statistics taken from July 1, 2007, U.S. Census Bureau estimates. Land and water area statistics taken from 2000 Census, U.S. Census Bureau.

Manufactured with paper containing at least 10% post-consumer waste

Library of Congress Cataloging-in-Publication Data

Smith, Rich, 1954-
  Mississippi / Rich Smith.
      p. cm. -- (The United States)
  Includes index.
  ISBN 978-1-60453-659-1
  1. Mississippi--Juvenile literature. I. Title.

  F341.3.S64 2010
  976.2--dc22
                              2008051715

Table of Contents

The Magnolia State

Mississippi is in the Deep South region of the United States. It is the birthplace and home of some of the most important authors in American literature. Also, much of modern American music was influenced by people and events in Mississippi.

Farmers across the country use ideas started in Mississippi to grow and harvest bountiful crops. Many people believe the best-tasting seafood is found only in Mississippi.

In the middle of the 1900s, it was said that the road to the moon passed through Mississippi. This is because of the state's important role in rocketry.

Riverboats take passengers up and down the Mississippi River.

Quick Facts

Name: Mississippi comes from the Chippewa (a Native American tribe) language. It means "great river," or "father of waters."

State Capital: Jackson

Date of Statehood: December 10, 1817 (20th state)

Population: 2,938,618 (31st-most populous state)

Area (Total Land and Water): 48,430 square miles (125,433 sq km), 32nd-largest state

Largest City: Jackson, population 175,710

Nickname: The Magnolia State or The Hospitality State

Motto: *Virtute et armis* (By Valor and Arms)

State Bird: Mockingbird

Petrified Wood

Magnolia
Tree

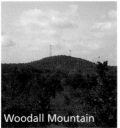

Woodall Mountain

State Flower: Magnolia

State Rock: Petrified Wood

State Tree: Magnolia

State Song: "Go, Mississippi"

Highest Point: 806 feet (246 m), Woodall Mountain

Lowest Point: 0 feet (0 m), Gulf of Mexico

Average July Temperature: 82°F (28°C)

Record High Temperature: 115°F (46°C) at Holly Springs, July 29, 1930

Average January Temperature: 48°F (9°C)

Record Low Temperature: -19°F (-28°C) at Corinth, January 30, 1966

Average Annual Precipitation: 58 inches (147 cm)

Number of U.S. Senators: 2

Number of U.S. Representatives: 4

U.S. Postal Service Abbreviation: MS

Geography

Mississippi is located along the coast of the Gulf of Mexico in the southern United States. Its neighbor to the north is Tennessee. To the east is Alabama. Louisiana and the Gulf of Mexico are to the south. The Mississippi River forms the state's western border. On the other side of the river are Arkansas and more of Louisiana.

The state of Mississippi covers 48,430 square miles (125,433 sq km). This makes it the 32nd-largest state in the United States.

Mississippi's land is mostly flat and low. It is divided into two parts. The first is the Delta region, in the northwest part of the state. It begins at the Mississippi River in the west and fans out toward the east. The soil of the Delta is a fertile loess.

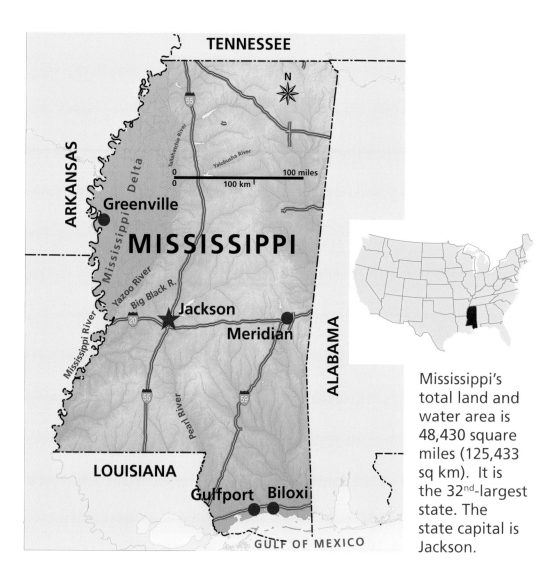

TENNESSEE

N

ARKANSAS

55

Tallahatchie River

Yalobusha River

100 miles

100 km

Greenville

Delta

Mississippi

MISSISSIPPI

Yazoo River

Big Black R.

Mississippi River

20

Jackson

Meridian

ALABAMA

55

59

Pearl River

LOUISIANA

Gulfport   Biloxi

GULF OF MEXICO

Mississippi's total land and water area is 48,430 square miles (125,433 sq km). It is the 32nd-largest state. The state capital is Jackson.

The second part of Mississippi is called the Gulf Coastal Plain. It begins at sea level and gradually rises toward the north. The highest point is only 806 feet (246 m) above sea level. That place is Woodall Mountain in the far northeastern corner of the state. The soil throughout much of the Gulf Coastal Plain is among the richest anywhere.

The state's important rivers besides the Mississippi include the Pearl, Big Black, Tallahatchie, Yalobusha, and Yazoo Rivers.

The Pearl River runs from about the middle of the state of Mississippi southward. It is the lower boundary between Mississippi and Louisiana.

Biloxi, Bay St. Louis, and Pascagoula are the three main bays along Mississippi's coastline. The shallow waters nearest the coast are known as the Mississippi Sound. The sound is separated from the deeper waters of the Gulf of Mexico by several barrier islands.

People enjoy Biloxi Beach, which borders the Gulf of Mexico.

Climate and Weather

Summers are very hot and humid in Mississippi. The average July temperature is about 82 degrees Fahrenheit (28°C). Winters are mild. The average January temperature is about 48 degrees Fahrenheit (9°C).

The reason for these temperatures is that Mississippi has a climate that is almost tropical. Mississippi climate is officially known as a subtropical climate. Subtropical climates also are usually wet. Mississippi receives 58 inches (147 cm) of rain each year.

Sometimes, Mississippi's rain is brought by hurricanes. Hurricanes do not strike Mississippi very often. But when they do, they cause much damage. Sea tides raised by these storms cause flooding far in from the shoreline because of the state's very low elevation.

Flooding also occurs along the Mississippi River because of rainfall many hundreds of miles north of the state. Mississippi also faces danger from tornadoes. An average of 24 tornadoes strike the state each year.

A professional storm chaser struggles to remain standing by clinging to a collapsing sign during the landfall of Hurricane Katrina in Gulfport, Mississippi, on August 29, 2005. The mess is still being cleaned up years later.

Plants and Animals

The most famous plant in Mississippi is the beautiful magnolia tree and its even more beautiful flower. That is one reason why the state chose the magnolia for its official tree and flower.

Other trees that grow in Mississippi include cypress, white oak, post oak, cottonwood, maple, elm, hickory, pecan, sweetgum, tupelo, and longleaf pine.

Magnolia

Cypress trees grow in swampy areas of Mississippi.

Mississippi's state wildflower is the coreopsis, or tickseed.

Among the state's wildflowers are the black-eyed Susan, Virginia creeper, Cherokee rose, Louisiana quillwort, pondberry, azalea, honeysuckle, bur marigold, cardinal flower, swamp rose mallow, partridge pea, and purple coneflower. Mississippi's state wildflower is the coreopsis, or tickseed.

Many kinds of animals live in Mississippi. There are black bears, coyotes, opossums, armadillos, minks, raccoons, striped skunks, rabbits, bats, mice, eastern indigo snakes, mole salamanders, and gopher frogs. The white-tailed deer and the red fox are the official state land mammals. The alligator is the official state reptile.

Winging their way across the skies of Mississippi are birds such as wrens, thrushes, warblers, red-cockaded woodpeckers, bald eagles, hawks, owls, loons, seagulls, wood storks, sandhill cranes, egrets, blue herons, brown pelicans and ospreys. The state's official bird is the mockingbird.

The waters of Mississippi are full of catfish, bass, perch, mullet, crayfish, shrimp, blue crab, flounder, and sea turtles. The bottlenose dolphin is the state's official water mammal. The largemouth bass is the official fish, and the oyster is the official seashell.

The white-tailed deer is one of Mississippi's official state land mammals.

Dolphin

Sandhill Cranes

Alligator

History

The first people to live in Mississippi arrived several thousand years ago. They formed 15 Native American tribes. The most important were the Choctaw, Chickasaw, Natchez, Biloxi, and Yazoo.

In 1540, Hernando de Soto passed through the Mississippi area.

European explorers came to Mississippi in the middle 1500s. Hernando de Soto of Spain passed through in 1540 in search of treasures. He never found any.

France claimed Mississippi for itself in the 1680s. The first French settlement was built in 1699 near what now is the city of Biloxi. Other settlements were built soon afterward at Natchez.

Pierre Le Moyne came ashore in Mississippi in 1699. He built a fort near today's Biloxi.

France went to war with Great Britain and lost Mississippi in 1763. Britain in turn lost it to Spain during America's War of Independence. Spain gave the area to the United States in the late 1790s. The United States named it Mississippi Territory in 1798. The territory was divided in half in 1817. The eastern half became Alabama Territory. The western half became the state of Mississippi. It was the 20th state admitted to the Union.

Only one-third of Mississippi at the time of statehood was settled by white people. The rest of the state was the home of the Choctaw and Chickasaw Native American tribes. Beginning in the 1820s, the United States forced those tribes off their lands and made them move west to Oklahoma. The emptied tribal lands were then taken by cotton farmers. The farmers used African slaves to tend the fields and pick the cotton.

Mississippi plantation owners used African slaves to tend the fields and pick cotton.

Mississippi's economy depended so much on slavery that the state went to war in 1861 to keep it. The United States said slavery

The 1863 Vicksburg battle was a turning point for Union success.

had to end. But Mississippi and 10 other Southern states refused to obey. The Southern states formed their own country. They called it the Confederate States of America. The war between the United States and the Confederacy was known as the American Civil War. It lasted until 1865. One of the war's most important battles took place at Vicksburg, Mississippi, in 1863. The Confederacy lost the battle. The defeat led to the Confederacy losing the entire war.

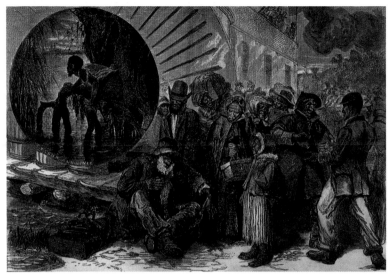

Before the Civil War, people escaped slavery by running away (round inset). After the war, slaves were free. They could come and go as they chose. However, many still faced mistreatment for years to come.

The slaves of Mississippi were set free after the Civil War. Mississippi was then brought back into the United States. But the former slaves were treated badly by the former slave owners and their descendants. The mistreatment continued for the next 100 years, until the United States passed laws putting a stop to it. Many African Americans left the state long before then. Starting in the early 1900s, they moved by the thousands to the big cities of the Northern states.

Whites and blacks came together after the civil rights movement of the 1960s to help make Mississippi a state where people of all colors can live in peace and prosperity.

In the 1960s, Mississippi became an important part of America's efforts to travel to the moon. That helped the state begin to modernize.

The Mississippi Test Facility, now called the Stennis Space Center, was used to test parts of the Saturn V rocket in 1967.

Did You Know?

- The idea behind the invention of the Teddy bear came from an event that happened in Mississippi. President Theodore Roosevelt in 1902 went to the state to hunt bears. A newspaper poked fun of that hunting trip by publishing a cartoon showing Roosevelt with a cute little bear instead of a ferocious one. A toy maker in New York saw the cartoon and was inspired by it. He called his new toy a Teddy bear because Roosevelt's nickname was Teddy.

1899-1902

- The popular soft drink Coca-Cola was invented in 1886. For about eight years afterwards, it was sold only at drug stores from a soda fountain. The first to put Coca-Cola in a bottle was a candy company in Vicksburg, Mississippi.

- The coldest it has ever been in subtropical Mississippi was -19 degrees Fahrenheit (-28°C). That happened on January 30, 1966, in the town of Corinth.

People

Jim Henson (1936-1990) was the creator of the Muppets. He made his first puppets for a children's television show while he was still in high school. It was in college that he came up with the  idea for his most famous character, Kermit the Frog. Henson's Muppets appeared regularly on *Sesame Street* and later had their own hit TV series called *The Muppet Show*. They also starred in several motion pictures. All of this helped make Henson one of the most successful puppeteers in American entertainment history. He was born in Greenville, Mississippi.

James Earl Jones (1931-) owns the deep voice you hear when *Star Wars*'s Darth Vader speaks from behind his mask. Jones is an award-winning film actor who has starred in many movies. One important role was in the television mini-series *Roots: The Next Generations*. The successful actor also has won awards for his stage performances. Jones was born in Arkabutla.

Brett Favre (1969-) is one of the most successful National Football League quarterbacks in history. He played for the University of Southern Mississippi for four years. Favre is most well known as the starting quarterback for the Green Bay Packers. From 1992-2007, he led the Packers to many division championships, as well as a Super Bowl win in 1997. Favre was born in Gulfport.

Elvis Presley (1935-1977) helped make rock and roll music popular in the 1950s. He then went on to become one of the most famous musicians in the world. That is why his nickname is The King. Presley played guitar and piano and had a powerful singing voice. He also starred in many movies. His name has been added to four major music halls of fame. Presley was born in Tupelo, Mississippi.

William Faulkner (1897-1962) was an important novelist who wrote mainly about people and life in Mississippi. His works are considered classics of American literature. The most beloved Faulkner stories are *The Sound and the Fury*, *As I Lay Dying*, and *Light in August*. Faulkner won a Nobel Prize for literature in 1949. He was born in New Albany.

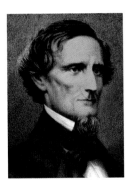

Jefferson Davis (1808-1889) was the first and only president of the rebel Confederate States of America during the Civil War. Before that, he was a United States senator representing Mississippi. He also served as secretary of war for President Franklin Pierce. Davis was born in Kentucky, but spent most of his childhood near Woodville.

Cities

Jackson is the capital of Mississippi. It is also the state's most populous city. Its population is approximately 175,710. Jackson's nickname is Crossroads of the South. It is located in the western half of southern Mississippi. Jackson started as a trading village called LeFleur's Bluff. It became Jackson in 1822 when it was renamed in honor of President Andrew Jackson. The biggest businesses in the city today are makers and distributors of metal products, machinery, electronics, and packaged food.

The second-most populated city in Mississippi is **Gulfport**. It has an estimated population

Gulfport's deep-water port hosts many ships.

of 66,271. Gulfport is located along the state's Gulf of Mexico coast. Its miles of white sand beaches are famous around the world. So is its large, deep-water port. The city was founded in 1898. Much of it was ruined in 2005 by Hurricane Katrina. Today, Gulfport is repairing the damage and is coming back bigger and better than ever.

Biloxi is Mississippi's third-most populous city. It has an estimated 44,292 residents. The city is known as the Seafood Capital of the World. Biloxi was founded in 1699 a few miles east of what is now the city of Ocean Springs. Biloxi officially has been at its current location since 1838. The city today has many beachfront casinos and other shops that support tourism.

Tubs of shrimp from the Gulf of Mexico.

The famous Biloxi Lighthouse, built in 1848, survived the winds of 2005's Hurricane Katrina.

The largest city in Mississippi up until 1930 was **Meridian**. Today, it is the fourth-most populous city. Its population is 38,314. Meridian formerly was one of the South's biggest manufacturing centers. Meridian is located in the middle part of the state, near the Alabama border.

Greenville is located on the western border of Mississippi. It sits next to a lake that formed when the Mississippi River changed course long ago. The population of Greenville is about 36,178.

Transportation

The longest and busiest inland waterway in the nation is the Mississippi River.

Many barges transport goods on the Mississippi River.

The cities of Greenville, Vicksburg, Natchez, and Rosedale, plus the county of Yazoo, operate important ports along the river. Waterways also connect the Mississippi, Tennessee, and Ohio Rivers to the state's two deepwater Gulf of Mexico seaports at Gulfport and Pascagoula.

Since 1987, Mississippi has worked to add an extra 1,700 miles (2,736 km) of four-lane highway to its already very good system of roads.

Passenger trains stop in Mississippi along the Chicago-to-New Orleans route, and also along the route between New

A train bridge crosses the Mississippi River at Vicksburg, Mississippi.

Orleans, Louisiana, and Atlanta, Georgia. Freight trains use 2,000 miles (3,219 km) of track that crisscross the state.

Seven major commercial airports offer service in and out of Mississippi. The busiest are Gulfport-Biloxi International and Jackson-Evers International Airports.

Natural Resources

Mississippi has more than 11 million acres (4.5 million ha) of farmland. Farms in the state make the most money raising chickens. Other important farm products include cotton, soybeans, and beef.

A catfish in shallow water.

More than 70 percent of the catfish eaten in the United States comes from Mississippi. Commercial fishermen in the Gulf of Mexico pull in nets filled with shrimp, blue crab, mullet, and red snapper.

Much lumber each year comes from the 18 million acres (7.3 million ha) of forests in Mississippi. The thickest forests are found in the southeastern part of the state.

The mines of Mississippi produce Fuller's earth, clay, bentonite, crushed stone, and industrial sand and gravel.

A cotton picker harvests a field on a farm near Clarksdale, Mississippi.

Industry

In October 2000, a terrorist bomb left the USS *Cole* with a huge hole in its side. The Navy destroyer was repaired at the Ingalls Shipyard in Pascagoula, Mississippi.

Mississippi manufactures many useful products such as ships and cars. The city of Pascagoula has a large shipyard where merchant freighters and Navy warships are put together. The city of Canton, near Jackson, has a gigantic factory that builds Nissan automobiles and trucks.

Stennis Space Center conducts a test on a hybrid rocket motor.

A test firing on the A-1 Test Stand. Stennis tests space shuttle engines.

Another important industry in Mississippi is space flight research. The state is home to the John C. Stennis Space Center, located in southern Mississippi. This is the nation's largest facility for the testing of rocket engines. The thrusters that hurl NASA's space shuttle into orbit are tested here.

Gambling is big business these days in Mississippi. The state legalized casino gambling in 1990. This led to a boom in the construction of casinos and hotels around the state.

Sports

In Mississippi, minor-league sports are a major attraction, since there are no big-league teams in the state. One of the most popular minor-league teams is the Mississippi Sea Wolves. They are a hockey team from Biloxi. The state's other hockey team is the Mississippi RiverKings of Southaven.

Based in the city of Pearl are the Mississippi Braves. They are a minor-league "farm team" for Major League Baseball's Atlanta Braves.

Mississippi residents love college football. The team from the University of Mississippi is called the Rebels.

The Rebels have millions of loyal fans. So do the teams from Mississippi State University (the Bulldogs) and the University of Southern Mississippi (the Golden Eagles).

Many people from Mississippi enjoy outdoor sports. Recreational activities include hunting, fishing, swimming, boating, sailing, canoeing, waterskiing, camping, hiking, bicycling, and more.

A fisherman holds up his catch. Fishing is a popular sport in Mississippi.

Entertainment

Music is an important part of life in Mississippi. This is the state where the musical style known as the blues began. From the blues came jazz, rock and roll, bluegrass, rhythm and blues, and other modern styles. Music scholars in 2005 began putting up markers where important events in blues history occurred. These markers form what is called the Mississippi Blues Trail.

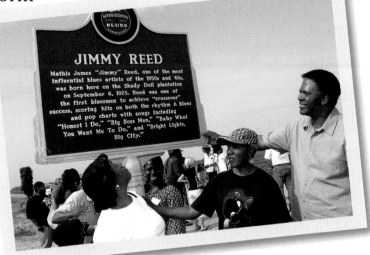

A Mississippi Blues Trail Marker honors musician Jimmy Reed.

The marker reads:

JIMMY REED

Mathis James "Jimmy" Reed, one of the most influential blues artists of the 1950s and '60s, was born here on the Shady Dell plantation on September 6, 1925. Reed was one of the first bluesmen to achieve "crossover" success, scoring hits on both the rhythm & blues and pop charts with songs including "Honest I Do," "Big Boss Man," "Baby What You Want Me To Do," and "Bright Lights, Big City."

Mississippi also is home to several fine symphony orchestras and dance troupes. The USA International Ballet Competition is held once every four years in Jackson.

USA International Ballet Competition dancers in a flag ceremony representing 24 countries and almost 100 competitors in Jackson, Mississippi.

Among the state's most celebrated authors are John Grisham, Tennessee Williams, Alice Walker, and Eudora Wells. Their books join more than 5 million others on the shelves of Mississippi's many public libraries.

There are many museums in Mississippi. They display everything from dinosaur skeletons to modern art.

Timeline

5000 BC—First humans arrive in Mississippi. They later group into 15 Native American tribes.

1540—Hernando de Soto of Spain travels through Mississippi.

1699—Explorer Pierre Le Moyne of France establishes the first European settlement in Mississippi.

1798—Spain gives up control of Mississippi to the United States. Mississippi becomes a U.S. territory.

1817—Mississippi becomes the 20th state admitted to the Union.

1820s—Native Americans are forced to leave the state. White farmers take over the former Indian lands. Cotton becomes an important crop. Slavery spreads.

1861—Mississippi leaves the U.S. in order to keep slavery legal. The Civil War begins.

1865—The Confederacy is defeated. Slaves are freed.

1900s—Many African Americans flee Mississippi to escape hardships.

1960s—U.S. Congress and courts pass laws to stop unfair treatment of African Americans. Mississippi begins to modernize.

2005—Hurricane Katrina brings death and destruction to Mississippi coastal towns.

Glossary

Barrier Island—A long, narrow landform just offshore from a mainland. Typically, a barrier island is made up of sand, silt, and pebbles.

Civil Rights Movement—A social movement in the United States in the 1960s. The civil rights movement tried to reduce discrimination and prejudice against African Americans and other racial minorities.

Delta—A triangular-shaped section of land formed from sediments where the mouth of a flowing river meets an ocean or other body of water. A delta can fan out over a distance of a few yards or many miles.

Descendant—A person whose ancestors trace back to some point in the past. Example: Jane's father is John, and John's mother is Sarah, which makes Jane a descendant of Sarah.

Hurricane—A violent windstorm that begins in tropical ocean waters and moves in a generally northerly direction. It begins to break up after it reaches land. But before that, it causes tides to rise dangerously high along shorelines and brings deadly waves, driving rain, and even tornadoes. Hurricanes often do great damage.

Loess—A German word that means "loose." A silty soil formed when rocks are eroded by glaciers and then carried long distances by wind. The loess of Mississippi is usually a yellowish-brown color.

National Aeronautics and Space Administration (NASA)—A U.S. government agency started in 1958. NASA's goals include space exploration, as well as increasing people's understanding of Earth, our solar system, and the universe.

Waterway—A stream or river wide and deep enough for boats to travel along.

Index